DIANE WALLER

textiles from
the balkans

THE BRITISH MUSEUM PRESS

The preparation of this publication was generously supported by the Sosland Family, Kansas City, through the American Friends of the British Museum.

First published in 2010 by The British Museum Press
A division of The British Museum Company Ltd
38 Russell Square, London WC1B 3QQ

www.britishmuseum.co.uk

Diane Waller has asserted the right to be identified as the author of this work

A catalogue record for this book is available from the British Library

ISBN: 978-0-7141-2583-1

Designer: Price Watkins
Map: Technical Art Services
Printed by C&C Offset, China

The names and designations used on the map on p. 21 do not imply official endorsement or acceptance by the British Museum.

Cover: Detail from a woman's sleeveless jacket. (See pages 38–9)
Inside cover: Detail from a woman's apron, Pleven, Bulgaria.
Previous pages: Detail from a carpet, Chiprovtski, Bulgaria. (See pages 46–7)
These pages: Details from women's socks, Sofia region, Bulgaria. (See pages 44–5)

contents

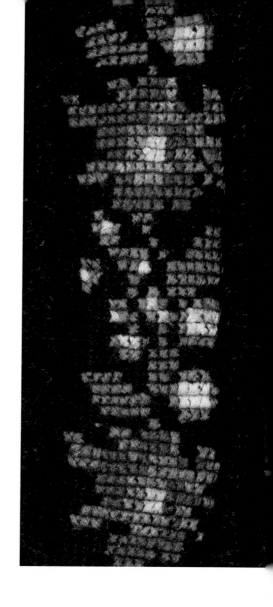

introduction

The Balkans are a complex mosaic of ethnic, religious and cultural groups, each with their distinct traditions that cross national frontiers. The name originally came from the Balkan Mountains, running through the centre of Bulgaria into eastern Serbia. The Balkans now cover a broader geographical area, which includes many of the countries in Southeastern Europe (see the map on p. 21). It is mountainous region that stands at the crossroads between central Europe and the Near East.

Unified by freezing winters, very hot summers and poor-quality land, the people

from the Balkans traditionally suffered a harsh existence. Some of the most interesting textiles still bear the stains of daily labour, in the house, yard and field, and tell us much about the lives of the women and men who wore them. The regions also have a lot in common ethnographically, with costumes, dances, music and folk customs bearing the influences of the Slavs, Thracians, Proto-Bulgarians and Greeks of antiquity and the Middle Ages. Part of the Ottoman Empire for 500 years, it is not surprising therefore that there are significant Ottoman and Islamic influences in the Balkans (the Turks only relinquished control of Macedonia in 1912). Rich merchants were able to afford expensive fabrics such as silk and fur that were brought in from abroad, while the Orthodox Church inspired many beautiful monasteries and works of art. This diversity of influences is reflected in the textiles selected for this book, which include those from the former Yugoslavia (in particular the regions of Macedonia, Serbia, Montenegro and Kosovo), Albania, Greece and Bulgaria.

The British Museum's collection of Balkan textiles is exceptional, with many complete costumes and accompanying accessories. Most date from the beginning of the twentieth century to around the 1950s. Macedonian and Bulgarian textiles are the most numerous in the collection. There had been a few acquisitions in the nineteenth and early twentieth centuries, notably a handful of pieces from the distinguished traveller and writer Mary Edith Durham (1863–1944) in 1914,

but the nucleus of the collection was formed by a large gift made in 1971 from the Bulgarian Committee for Cultural Relations. Without specific documentation, it is often hard to date textiles. However, the 1990s saw the addition of large groups of material from collectors who had lived or worked in the Balkans and who kept meticulous documentation.

The Balkans proved a fascinating destination for a generation of women travellers. Many went for humanitarian reasons, including Mary Edith Durham and Rebecca West (1892–1983). At least four of the Museum's collectors were members of folklore groups (Yugoslav and Bulgarian), and bought the costumes to wear at presentations and performances to be as true as possible to the spirit of the dance and to the various styles of different regions (above right). Extremely heavy costumes were correct for the slow and dignified, even sombre, dances in some regions – for example, *nestinarka*, a Macedonian bride's dance, where the costume consisted of several layers of heavy woven and embroidered woollen garments covering an even more heavily embroidered linen dress (with accompanying layers of coin chains pinned to the bodice, silver belt buckles and head ornaments). In other regions, where the dances were fast and furious, lighter costumes were more appropriate, such as those from northern Bulgaria.

Nowadays traditional clothing is not considered suitable for everyday wear, except occasionally by older people in remote villages and small towns. With the rapid industrialization of the past forty years,

The author (third from left) with the Injevo women's dance group, East Macedonia.

the more lightweight, modern western-style dress, which is both easier to wear and to clean, has been adopted. Costumes that are worn to this day include 'Sunday best', and feast day wear. Traditionally feast days provided a necessary light relief to the harsh living conditions, as well as having a strong spiritual significance.

Items made today are mainly produced by co-operatives, for dance groups or for tourists, and tend to be of machine-made material and embroidery. There are still women who do hand-weaving and embroidery, making blouses, tablecloths, rugs and wall-hangings. But the older, hand-made costumes are very hard to come by now and will eventually only be seen in museums or on the stage at folk-dance festivals.

In the 1970s, a time of emigration, many families in Macedonia wanted to sell their costumes prior to emigrating to Australia. Others disposed of them because they represented a patriarchal society, or simply because they preferred to use the money to buy a television or a labour-saving device. The wish to purchase a television was the main reason given to the author by many elderly women keen to sell their clothes.

WEAVING

The basic skill needed to make textiles in this region was weaving. The textiles were made of hemp, linen and wool, with cotton used more recently, and occasionally silk. Traditionally cloth was woven on horizontal looms. The Pirot region of Serbia and Bulgaria's Chiprovtsi region are famous for their kilims (flat woven carpets) and goat-hair products. Households wove their own items for daily use, including rugs and kilims, and to decorate the home for special occasions, such as births, weddings and funerals. In Greece, during the eighteenth century, weaving developed into an organized industry in which men also took part. Across the Balkans, woven goods were an important aspect of commerce and export.

EMBROIDERY AND SEWING

This is both a highly skilled art form and an ancient tradition, showing influences from Byzantium and from medieval, Renaissance and Ottoman traditions. In traditional Bulgarian folk costume, for example, there are strictly defined areas for the application of embroidery. The centre of the embroidered decoration was that of the chemise, which formed the undergarment for most costume. Most of the embroidery was down the front and on the cuffs or hem, adding colour, pattern and shape to the garment.

Embroidery is done in two ways – either by counting the threads of the fabric, or by following a pattern drawn on the fabric in advance. Counting threads was the most prevalent method in the Balkans. Stitches most frequently used were cross, oblique, straight, split and knotted, while materials included linen, cotton, wool and silk, with a predominance of woollen threads on woollen parts of the costumes in mountainous regions. Plaited woollen cords were couched onto garments in very elaborate patterns. In Greece, couched metal thread embroidery was undertaken by professional tailors, many of them Jewish, living in Skopje, Yanina (Joánnina), Thessaloniki and elsewhere. Such embroidered clothing is characteristic of the Balkans. Silk was used in those regions where the silkworm was bred and was a valuable export. Openwork effects were created by using either drawn threadwork in which threads were removed, or pulled threadwork in which threads are teased apart. The remaining threads were then bound together (see pp. 64–5).

Mastery of sewing and embroidery was considered to be one of the most important qualities in a young woman, especially during her pre-marital life. The choice of a fiancée often largely depended on the number and artistic qualities of the clothes, embroidered garments and other elements of her dowry. Girls were required to make 'samplers' demonstrating their skills in a range of embroidery methods. Despite the custom of adhering to traditional patterns, it was considered an advantage to have improvisational skills.

PATTERNS AND COLOUR

Widely found in the Balkans are textiles with the ancient *rhomb* (diamond-shaped) design, simple or complicated geometrical forms, and hook-shaped motifs. The designs incorporate plant motifs, flowers, leaves and vines, and also animals, birds and insects (right). The making of kilims developed from the sixteenth and seventeenth centuries under Turkish influence. Some of the finest kilims are to be found in mosques throughout the region, and elsewhere in the world. In Serbia, Pirot, Šumadija, areas of Vojvodina and parts of the Pannonian plain were particularly important for kilim production, as were Chiprovtsi and Kotel in Bulgaria, and Kosovo. The kilims have similar patterns and colours – particularly the 'tree of life' motif (far right) – along with birds, plants and animals.

The dyes were originally of vegetable matter, which produced subtle shades of dark blue, brown, dark red and green. In Kosovo the kilims produced by ethnic Albanians also used black, dark brown, violet and yellow. From the nineteenth century these were replaced by chemical dyes, which were easier to prepare and gave a wider range of hue. Colours became cruder and brighter, and the introduction of *pembe* ('shocking pink') in particular proved very popular among the local population. Some kilims produced today are very gaudy, made out of poor materials and bearing little resemblance to the fine craftwork of the late nineteenth and early twentieth centuries.

WOMEN'S COSTUME

This section focuses on the diversity of women's costume to be found in the Balkans, followed by a closer look at the different regions.

The basic Slav costume was red, white and black, but, as with the kilims, the introduction of chemical dyes in the second half of the

Samakov sleeve with plant and root motifs, Bulgaria.

Samakov hem with 'tree of life' motif, Bulgaria.

nineteenth century gave a wider range of possibilities. Some of these dyes were also fast when washed in cold water, an important aspect for clothing. Underlying all Balkan costume is a complex belief system that dictated the type of garment and the decoration. The chemise, which forms the undergarment for most costumes, was made from flax (the raw material for linen) which was washed, beaten and hung or laid out in the sun to bleach – a sight which could still be seen in the 1970s by Lake Ohrid in Macedonia. The chemise or dress was heavily embroidered at the openings – the neck, sleeves and hem – to protect against the entry of evil spirits. Over the chemise, women wore a variety of different jackets or overdresses made of wool, linen or padded cotton. The jackets were usually decorated with couched braid or embroidered down the front and on the back and hem, sometimes with gold or silver metal-wrapped thread and with fur and velvet around the cuffs. They either wore one apron, wrapped round the lower half of the body, or two aprons, one often pleated at the back and the other straight, at the front (right). Like the embroidery, aprons were also believed to protect the body from evil spirits, which explains why they were worn at the back as well as the front. The woollen aprons of varying thicknesses had striking geometric patterning and stripes.

In another variety of costume, a sleeveless overdress of dark blue or black woollen material was worn over the chemise to about knee-length in order to reveal the embroidery on the bottom of the chemise. Some belts were woven on tablet looms, and sometimes women wore long belts, made from plaited woollen yarn stitched together, wrapped several times around the waist rather like a corset.

Throughout the regions costume, colour and embroidery were significant in demonstrating a person's social status as well as identifying their village or town. For example, certain ornaments were embroidered on a baby's first shirt, baptismal clothes, the child's clothes before puberty and after the onset of sexual maturity, the wedding costume and in clothing of older men and women. As women grew older, the colours and variety of costume diminished.

As more fabrics, braids and ornaments became available throughout the twentieth century, women added decorations to the basic embroidery – not always, in the author's opinion, to the aesthetic improvement of the costume. Sometimes the costumes were passed down from grandmother to granddaughter and underwent change in the form of additions of lace or crochet, ribbons, sequins and beads, in an attempt to personalize the design. Despite such amendments, the basic form of the costume

Costume from Vidin, Northern Bulgaria.

remained very much the same throughout the regions represented in this book, with the most striking features being the immense variety of style and detail.

The development of very beautiful and elaborate costumes was often not commensurate with the means or standard of living of the people. It was, however, seen as essential that a daughter should be correctly dressed, to avoid both her and her family being scorned when she left home. The family were prepared to incur large debts or even sell land to ensure they kept their good name.

In Greece there were three categories of costume – village style, oriental urban style and western urban style. Village style was usually made of hand-woven cloth. Cotton chemises were worn with overdresses (pinafore dresses) and woollen coats over the top, as found in Florina and the Karagouna costume of Thessaly. With elements made from more expensive material, the oriental urban style is seen in Yanina (Joánnina) and survived in Greek communities in Asia Minor I until the early twentieth century. The more modern western urban style of costume was typified by a long pleated dress of expensive silk cloth, which was worn on top of a cotton chemise. Either an embroidered woollen jacket or a felt waistcoat embroidered with fine gold braid was worn as a topcoat. According to Popi Zora from the Museum of Greek Folk Art in Athens, the naturalistic elements of Greek embroidery owed their origin to Persian influence. The basic form of plant-design is a survival of the oriental tree of life, usually portrayed as a large receptacle with flowers, flanked symmetrically by two animal or human figures. Other elements from Greek life and tradition, such as the snake, cock, double-headed eagle, mermaid, wedding scene, betrothal, bridal pair, musicians and dancers were also common.

Town costumes were also influenced by Western European fashions in some parts of Serbia, Montenegro and Bulgaria, and were made of expensive materials such as fine quality wool imported from Central Europe. In nineteenth-century Serbia and Kosovo, and in Bulgarian towns like Kotel and Kovprivchitsa, where many rich families were based, urban costume was usually made out of silk, velvet and fine linen, embroidered with silk or gold and silver thread, with jackets trimmed with fur. These costumes were often specially commissioned and made by tailors.

Across the Balkans, people in rural communities wore leather shoes made from one piece of leather, sometimes boar skin, shaped rather like a moccasin (see p. 14). Both men and women wore hand-knitted socks, either plain or with patterns. Geometric forms, flowers, animals, birds and insects were knitted into the body of the sock. Knitting was done on five needles, with socks decorated on the parts that were exposed to view. In the case of socks given as presents, the whole sock would be decorated. Each costume had its own headgear, ranging from a simple scarf to ornate silver and coin caps, or constructions of flowers, feathers and beads of 30 cm (14 in) high and over, worn for special occasions (see p. 15).

Jewellery was important throughout the Balkans, demonstrating the wearer's position in society. It was heavy, often of silver, in the form of huge silver buckles, chunky bracelets, necklaces, headbands and chains hung with coins, and silver coin-covered caps with streamers covered in more coins hanging down the back. Brides were required to wear as much jewellery as possible, and in some areas the custom required that she stand throughout her

Women from Kotel, central Bulgaria at a festival.

The Middle Ages also left a rich legacy, including about a hundred churches and monasteries with wall paintings of considerable beauty. During the Ottoman period Macedonian architecture absorbed many Turkish elements, for example, the mosque, the *tekija* (a Muslim monastery), the *haman* (a Turkish bath) and the *han* (a roadside inn or caravanserai). The designs and styles of the textiles from this region reflect the variety of cultural influences.

The folk-songs of the region bear witness to suffering in a land that is mountainous and harsh, and, not least the fact that men were unable to earn a living in their homeland and were forced to go abroad in search of work. Such circumstances naturally affected local customs and festivals. While in other regions weddings were usually scheduled for autumn after the harvest, in Galichnik and Lazaropolje they took place in summer during the same short period each year when the men returned.

wedding day and the following night (during which time the bridegroom slept) weighted down by the heavy costume and jewellery which formed part of her dowry. The wedding costumes of villagers from Galičhnik in Macedonia are particularly noteworthy in this respect, as are the costumes worn by the Sarakatsan, a nomadic people of Greek origin living throughout the region. Their striking costumes are predominantly dark red, blue and black, with heavy dark woven pleated skirts and luxuriously decorated jackets and aprons.

In Macedonia, the popular arts have always been rich and varied. Ancient ruins and relics shed light on the life of the early Balkan people and the later Greek and Roman civilizations.

Patterned socks and boar skin shoes, Injevo village, Macedonia.

14

A Young woman at St Lazarus' day festival, Sliven, Lazarka, Buglaria.

(dances) were either in a circle or a line. The ability to dance well was an asset in gaining a spouse. The women's dances showed modesty and reserve, with seniority being determined by the length of time a woman had been married, rather than by age.

Embroidery from the region of Galičnik is among the finest in the British Museum collection. It is predominately red, with small elements of yellow, made using pulled or drawn threadwork. The costumes are multi-layered, with the unmarried women wearing a somewhat simpler thick wool overjacket pleated at the back. Jackets are typically embellished with a multitude of decorative gold filigree buttons, as can be found on all three of the jackets that make up the costume on pp. 64–5.

One particular flower motif, which often appears on the embroidery is traditionally associated with the historic battle, that took place between the Turks and the Serbs on the plains of Kosovo in 1389. It is still commemorated to this day and plays an important role in popular traditions and in literature, especially in the epic poems of the Kosovo cycle. The poets sing of the courage of the Serbian fighters, who lost the battle. Legend has it that thousands of peonies grew up from the blood of the warriors who died there. The embroidered red hues symbolize the bloodshed, while the dark colours framing the red represent the nation's sorrow at losing its freedom.

The mountainous character of most of Serbia makes agriculture difficult. On the alternately baking and freezing plain between Belgrade and Zagreb, one can see little but sweetcorn and

Wedding festivites lasted up to a week. There were traditional songs, music and dances for every part of the wedding – the bride welcoming the guests, the bridegroom departing from his home, his return with the bride, her step over the threshold of her new home and her meeting with the bridegroom's family. The traditional *kolo*

melons growing. In the south, tobacco was an important export, as were carpets – particularly the kilims of Pirot – and pottery. The typical costume consisted of the *zubun* (a long, sleeveless coat open at the front), the *jelik* (short waistcoat), the *kecelja* (apron) and a fine chemise embroidered on the collar, sleeves and hem. The *jelik* was usually made of black or blue wool, and embroidered with braid or silver. The apron was made the same way, with its embroidery often being of flowers. In the British Museum collection there is a back apron of finely pleated material, which may be pulled up at the back into a 'butterfly' shape (right). This is both decorative and practical when working in muddy areas. A woven belt and embroidered socks complete the outfit.

For Muslim girls, the traditional costume comprised several metres of material, usually brocade, in a large square, folded in half and gathered into the waist, with a gap at each corner for the legs. The centre part was lifted and tucked into the waistband to give the appearance of trousers, with a *jelik* embroidered with gold or silver or pearls, and a blouse of fine silk. Wedding costumes were particularly richly decorated with a predominance of gold. These costumes were appropriate for the dances of certain regions – for example, the towns of Vranje and Prizren – which were performed by the women in an elegant and dignified manner, characterized by measured steps and gentle arm movements.

The costumes from around Djakovchitsa, a town in Kosovo not far from Prizren and noted

Back and rear views of Serbian aprons.

for its craftsmen, were quite different. Worn by ethnic Albanians, they comprised a white voluminous linen chemise, colourful front and back aprons and elaborate headgear. Prizren was for many years a prosperous centre of crafts and trade, an important product being filigree jewellery made from silver and gilt wire. Traditional techniques and ancient tools are still used, and Prizren filigree is highly prized locally and as an export commodity. Albanian influence is strongly felt in the region of Montenegro, in the coastal areas of Bar and Ulcinj. Here, Catholics, Orthodox and Muslim populations lived in harmony, with Muslims preserving many customs and costumes up until the 1970s. At Muslim weddings in this region, both Muslim and Montenegrin folk dances could be seen. The weddings were attended by several hundred people and picturesque costumes were worn.

MEN'S COSTUME

Throughout the region men's costumes were much simpler than the women's, usually consisting of a shirt that was embroidered at the neck, down the front and on the cuffs, thick baggy woollen trousers, and a woven sash, jackets and woollen socks. In Northern Bulgaria, men wore boots or clogs rather than leather shoes. In parts of Macedonia and in the Pirin region of Bulgaria and in Greece, the men wore a long white linen knee-length chemise over white linen or wool trousers, with a tightly wrapped sash over the chemise giving the impression of a skirt. In the mountainous Marievo region of Macedonia, a pleated apron-skirt was worn over thick woollen trousers and richly patterned socks (see p. 14).

Men's town costumes could be more elaborate, especially those of the rich merchants who copied the customs of the ruling power. Their jackets could be thickly trimmed with fur and embroidered in silver and gold thread, and their cloaks could be of brocade and velvet.
In the countryside, in winter men wore heavy sheepskin coats or woollen cloaks and fur or sheepskin hats. Likewise shepherds wore heavy cloaks with hoods forming a point above the head. In Kosovo, the Albanian men still wear their thick, felted white wool costumes, consisting of braided cream jackets and trousers and white felted hats, even in summer. Being more practical for work on the land, warm in the winter and quite elegant, men's traditional costume may also still be found in some rural areas in Serbia, whereas traditional women's costumes have rarely been found outside the museums from the 1960s onwards. In the 1970s a tailor in Chachak still regularly made men's costumes for everyday wear: thick blue wool, smart braided waistcoat, slightly baggy trousers and a woollen cap. No similar service was available for women, who had by that time fully adopted western dress.

THE ROLE OF CLOTHING IN CUSTOMS AND FESTIVALS

Most of the costumes collected would have been worn at festivals, but it is not possible to do justice here to the range of customs, rituals and festivals to be found throughout the Balkans, in the past or even today. In the section on women's costume we have seen the importance of certain rites of passage. From pre-marriage through to death, costumes reflected the age and social status of the population. In the regions where the Orthodox Church was influential, saints' days were commemorated and accompanied by rituals. These were also 'name days', reflecting the popular custom of naming people after saints – instead of celebrating their birthdays, people celebrated their saint's day. Festivals of folk song and dance are still popular, for example in Kovprivchitza and Pirin in Bulgaria (see p. 19).

Much of the information in this section is based on Mercia MacDermott's authoritative accounts. She spent more than twenty years living and working in Bulgaria, mainly in the 1960s to 1980s, and has written in detail about the customs of everyday life, many of which are also found in parts of the former Yugoslavia and Greece. Her impressive textiles and other items from Bulgaria are now part of the British Museum collection.

Kukeri costumes, from Voinyarovo, near Karlovo, central Bulgaria, showing elaborate head-dresses.

Christening and Childhood

Traditionally, the baby's godfather played the central role at a christening. A key duty of the godfather was to provide the child's first proper clothes and wrappings, together with a *povoi* (a long cord of plaited red and white threads, with a gold or silver coin and a blue bead on the ends, to bind the child's swaddling clothes). The clothes and *povoi* were made by the godmother.

At the christening, babies wore little caps decorated with red threads and coins. Clothes were very important markers of each stage of a child's life. When a baby began to crawl, added to their basic shirt would be leggings, a kind of kilt made of a piece of woollen material with a cord on its upper edge to tie it round the waist, and a little coat. This was the usual form of dress for both boys and girls until the age of three, and sometimes even until six or seven. They would then progress to wearing a little dress with a gathered skirt under their shirts, or just a longish shirt and a waistcoat.

The first time a girl put on full folk costume was a very important milestone in her life, and it would occur on reaching puberty. Since she had spun, woven, cut, sewn and decorated every item herself, the costume served as a visual testimony to her skill and maturity. It would be examined, discussed and assessed by her peers and all the women of the village, including those looking for a daughter-in-law. A girl's first appearance in her adult costume would be at one of the major spring festivals, such as St Lazarus' Day (see p. 15), St George's Day or Easter. This would be the day that the girl was allowed to join in the village dance for the first time, and thus she ceased to be a little girl and was now officially ready for betrothal. A boy's coming of age would be marked just before Christmas, when for the first time he would put on an embroidered shirt, braided trousers and a long woollen sash, and join a group of carol singers. He too could now join in the village dances and start looking for a bride.

Girls at Pirin festival,
Bulgaria.

The *Sedyanka*

At a time when boys and girls were strictly
segragated, the *sedyanka* was a gathering where
young people could meet a prospective partner in
a safe place (see p. 20). This was a society where
marriage was seen as essential. The girls would
meet at a friend's home, wearing their best
costumes and bringing work with them such as
spinning, sewing or embroidery. The boys would
arrive later, play music, tell stories and join in the
dancing. In many villages in the Balkans, aspects of
the *sedyanka* are still followed. *Sedyanki* took place
in autumn or winter. On the evening of the first
sedyanka of the season, the girls would gather
outside the village at a crossroads. This symbolized
the many paths that the boys might take on
leaving home, and the ensuing ritual of lighting a
fire and saying words involving each girl's favourite

boy was to ensure that all roads led the boys to
the *sedyanka*.

Betrothal

Although the young people's wishes were
generally taken into account, the parents
arranged the marriage, with the initiative
coming from the boy's family. Matchmakers
would normally be employed to make enquiries.
Parents were more interested in the girl's
willingness and ability to work than in her
looks. Good health, industriousness, a good
character and unblemished reputation were
essential qualifications, together with
excellence in domestic skills – not least
because the girl would have to complete
her trousseau. This was a huge undertaking,
comprising several sets of clothing, household

goods, numerous socks, aprons and shirts, as well as towels to be presented to guests at the wedding. The boy would normally have to do military service or build a new house. While the girl's family needed to have a good name and the boy to come from a good family, it seems as if the primary qualification for the boy was that he should not be a drunkard!

Marriage

Elaborate rituals were involved in the preparations for the marriage, and at the actual wedding itself, as we have seen in the section on women's costume. The rituals continued after marriage too – for example, in parts of the Former Yugoslavia the bridal attire was worn every Sunday until the birth of the first child. Throughout the regions, whether in those influenced by the Orthodox Church or by Islam, marriages were highly important events as economic stability depended on a prosperous union of families.

TRIUMPH OF CREATIVITY

This introduction can only scrape the surface of what is a truly amazing example of creativity, a brief testimony to the cultural complexity of the Balkans and to a bygone age that has been destroyed by the traumatic events of the twentieth century, in the form of both war and industrialization.

The collectors have looked after the items carefully, and the textiles in this book show the skill and the beauty of the work, and allows us to appreciate the history, culture and everyday lives of the people who made them.

Girls at a *sedyanka*, Chirpan, Burgaria.

TRIBAL SLIPPERS
Northern Albania, 1912

Edith Durham records receiving these hand-knitted slippers from Gruda tribesmen in the mountainous area of North Albania in 1912, 'in return for aid to burnt-out villages'. Durham was one of the great women travellers in the Balkans in the early 1900s. Her *High Albania*, published in 1909, remains a standard text to this day. Made of hand-spun wool, these slippers are decorated with commercial black braiding at the top, with a large applied motif with couched gold-coloured metal-wrapped thread.
33 × 16 cm (13¼ × 6½ in)

THE DECORATION ON THE ARCH OF THE SHOE BREAKS UP THE OTHERWISE PLAIN STOCKING STITCH. ITS CENTRAL POINT ECHOES THE POINTED TOE, TONGUE AND HEEL, AND THE OPENING IS FASTENED BY A PINK BUTTON.

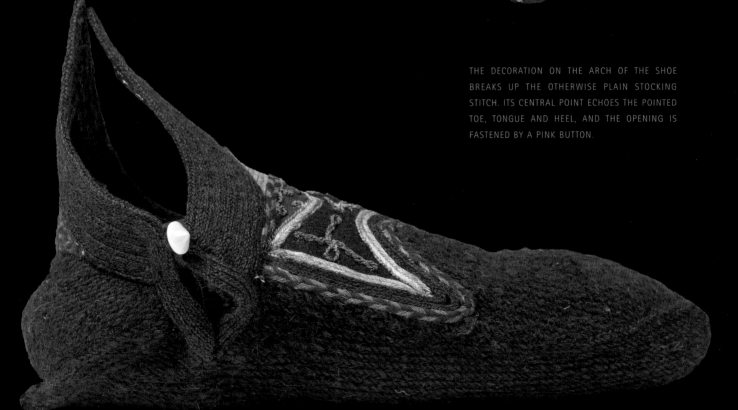

WOMAN'S HEADBAND
Albania, early 20th century

Women's headbands were worn vertically.
They have a pointed end at the bottom and
the top is raised and stiffened with paper.
Here, a pink cotton velvet
ground fabric is decorated with 'S',
'C' and flower-shaped motifs.
64 × 9.5 cm (25 1/4 × 3 3/4 in)

THE MOTIFS ARE WORKED WITH COUCHED GOLD- AND SILVER-COLOURED METAL-WRAPPED THREAD,
BRASS SEQUINS AND A FEW PURPLE AND GREEN SEQUINS.

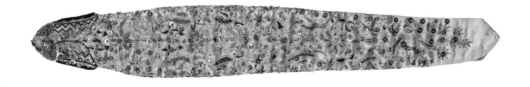

WOMAN'S HEADBAND
Albania, early 20th century

A lemon yellow satin silk ground is heavily decorated with couched embroidery and brass sequins with small coral beads attached. The headband is lined with two yellow fabrics: a golden yellow silk damask with a stemmed flower pattern, and a plain lemon yellow twill fabric.

64 × 9.5 cm (25 1/4 × 3 3/4 in)

DAISY-LIKE FLOWERS, TULIPS AND OTHER FOLIATE SHAPES ARE WORKED IN COUCHED GOLD-COLOURED METAL-WRAPPED THREAD AND GREEN, BLUE, PINK, RED AND PURPLE SILK EMBROIDERY.

EMBROIDERED APRON
Djakovchitsa, Kosovo, 1970s

This Albanian woman's apron was part of everyday summer clothing. It is made from
four separate fabrics: two pieces of purple cotton cloth and two pieces of black crocheted cloth.
The front (below) has a fringed band of open crochet above a patterned centre, while the back
(right) has a large 'S'-shaped motif made of glass beads.
37 × 52.5 cm (14²/₃ × 20²/₃ in)

THE ELABORATELY EMBROIDERED CENTRE HAS FLORAL PATTERNING WORKED IN
BLACK AND PURPLE SILK AND TEN CLUSTERS OF BLACK AND WHITE BEADS.

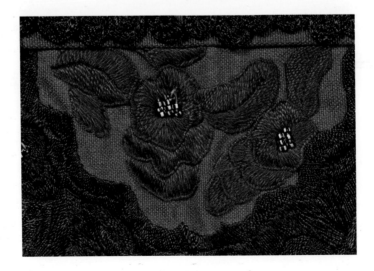

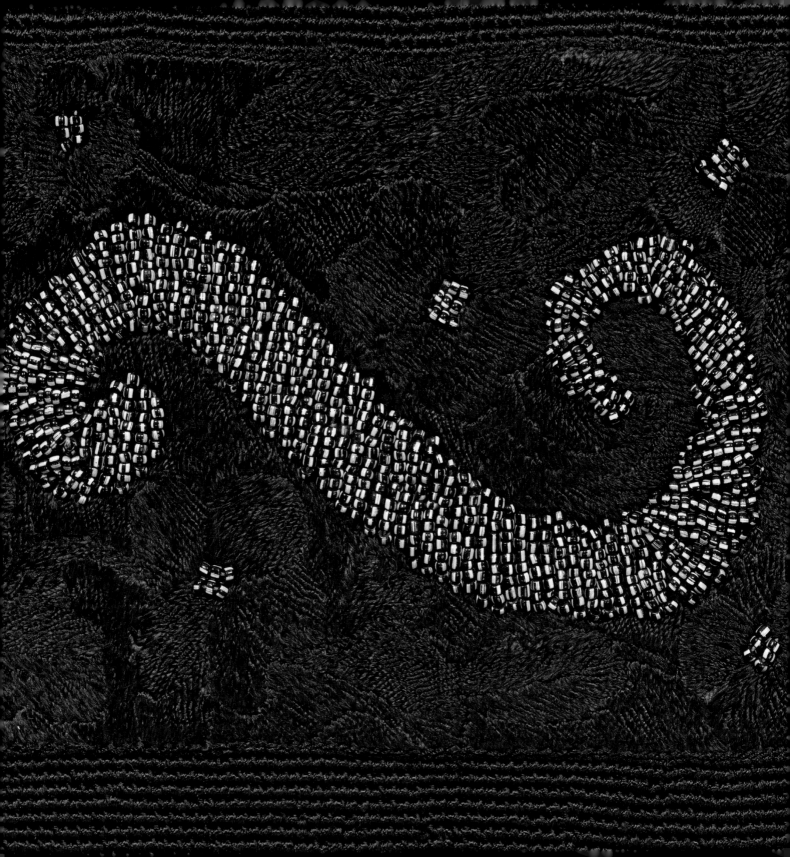

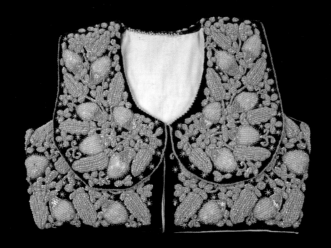

DEEP RED COTTON VELVET IS
COVERED IN PARTLY PADDED
EMBROIDERY AND ELABORATE
COUCHING.

THE FLOWER AND LEAF
MOTIFS ARE WORKED IN PALE
PINK PEARLS, SEQUINS AND
GOLD-COLOURED BRAIDING.

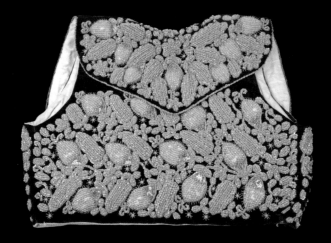

WEDDING WAISTCOAT
Albania, early 20th century

This Albanian woman's waistcoat is part of an urban Muslim
wedding outfit, which includes trousers, a wrap-around skirt,
an apron, a blouse and a headcloth.
35 × 47 cm (13³⁄₄ × 18¹⁄₂ in)

THE CUFFS AND THE COLLARS ARE DELICATELY EMBROIDERED
WITH MULTI-COLOURED SYNTHETIC WOOL AND COTTON YARNS,
WITH A CROCHETED TRIM ON THE SLEEVES.

MAN'S SHIRT (*ZADRIME*)
Albania, early 20th century

This everyday shirt is knee-length, and is made of cream and beige
striped cotton cloth. It is made up of several panels: the one for the front and
back use the full width, two for each sleeve and two for each side gusset. The
wide sleeves are set at right-angles and gathered into a deep cuff.
97 × 156 cm (38 1/4 × 61 1/2 in) with sleeves spread out

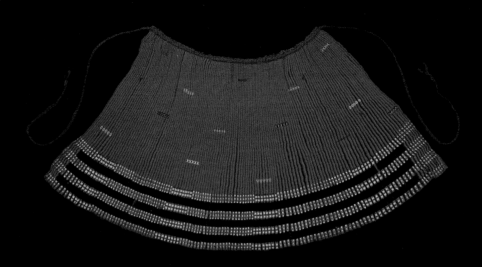

WOMAN'S BACK APRON (*VOLNENIK*)
Village of Boinitsa, Vidin in north-east Bulgaria, early 20th century.

This apron of ancient Slav origin is made from one rectangular piece of fabric, using single red cotton warp threads. The material is gathered and stiched to secure the pleats, aided by the contrastingly coloured yarns used in the weft. The top of the apron is sewn onto a red woollen plaited braid, which also serves as the apron's ties.
57 × 126 cm (22 1/2 × 49 2/3 in), open

THE THREE BLACK COTTON VELVET BANDS APPLIED TO THE HEM PROVIDE A STRIKING CONTRAST TO THE MULTI-COLOURED EMROIDERY.

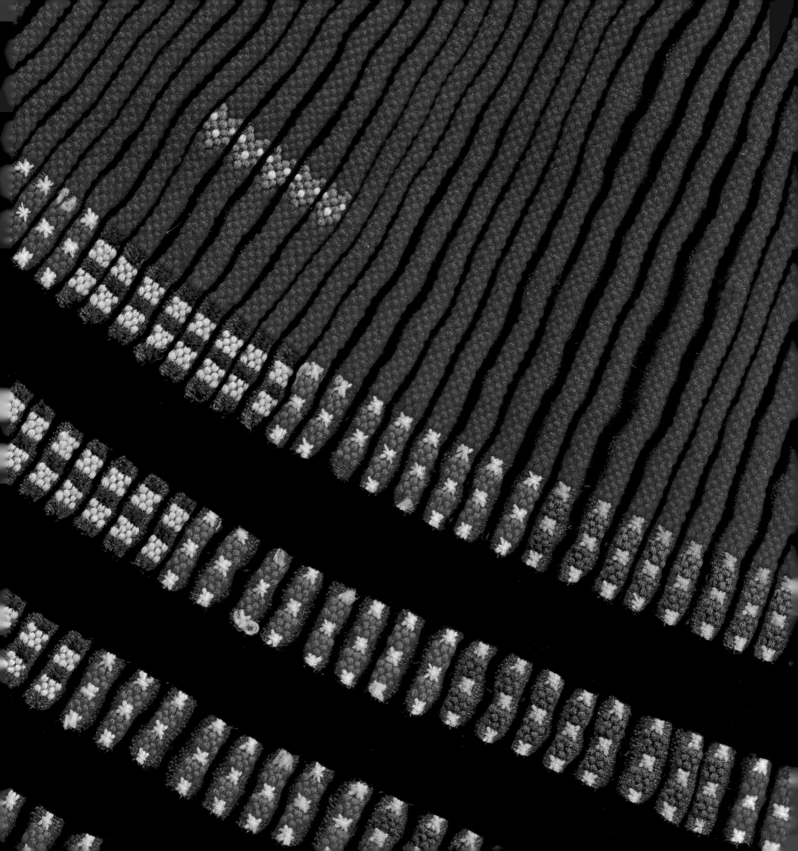

WOMAN'S CHEMISE (*BURCHANKA*)
Pleven, northern Bulgaria, late 19th century

This chemise from Pleven, northern Bulgaria, was worn for festivities.
Its name *burchanka* comes from the gathered neckline and sleeves.
The front and back central panels use the full weaving width, and the four side
panels create the A-line shape. The repeated motif on the hem (above) shows a
woman in a billowing skirt, worked in alternate black and red cross-stitch.
143 × 119 cm (56 1/3 × 47 in)

THE CHEST, COLLAR, SLEEVES AND HEMLINE ARE EMBROIDERED
USING HAND-SPUN COLOURED WOOLS. THE PATTERNS ARE
TYPICAL OF THOSE WORN BY YOUNG WOMEN OF MARRYING AGE.

WOMAN'S OUTER GARMENT (*SUKMAN*)

Govedartsi village, Samakov district, Bulgaria, late 19th century

Made of black woollen felted cloth, this garment has a scooped shaped neckline to reveal the embrodiered chemise worn beneath. The neckline is finely decorated with rows of multi-coloured chain stitch and has a small separate round collar. The red sleeves (right) are very densely decorated.

116 × 105 cm (45²/₃ × 41¹/₃ in)

THE SLEEVES HAVE A MIXTURE OF CHAIN STITCH AND BRIGHTLY COLOURED BRAIDING. THE MULTI-COLOURED HEM INCLUDES IMPORTED GOLD.

WOMAN'S SLEEVELESS JACKET (*GUNCHE*)
Pudarevo, Sliven district, Bulgaria, early 20th century

This is part of a festive dress for a young married woman. This outer garment is made from blue/black woven cloth. The U-shaped neckline is decorated with rows of blue wool braiding similar to that around the armholes.

56 × 66 cm (22 × 26 in)

THE VERMILION STITICHING ENHANCES THE ELEGANT DESIGN OF THIS JACKET.

WOMAN'S OUTER JACKET
Smolyan, Bulgaria, early 20th century

Trimmed with fur and with fine couched
embroidery at the neck opening, the breast
and on the cuffs, this jacket would have
been worn by a wealthy merchant's wife.
The embroidery features an endless knot and
flowing motifs based on plants – the designs
are identical on each side.
39.5 × 112 cm (15 $^2/_3$ × 44 in)

THE FLUID METAL-WRAPPED THREAD IS
COUCHED WITH YELLOW SILK.

WOMAN'S CHEMISE
Kyustendil, western Bulgaria,
early 20th century

This chemise is made of fine, but heavy, cream-coloured woven cloth containing a thin silk stripe. It would have been worn for best and festival days. Only the embroidered areas of the chemise would show from beneath the outer garment, which would have been similar to the one illustrated on pp. 36–7.
112 × 123 cm (44 × 48½ in)

THE INTRICATE GEOMETRIC MOTIFS INCLUDE IMPORTED GOLD THREAD.

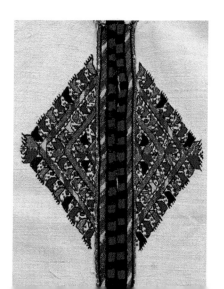

THE SLEEVE AND THE HEM HAS A SIMPLE RED AND BLACK CROCHETED EDGE.

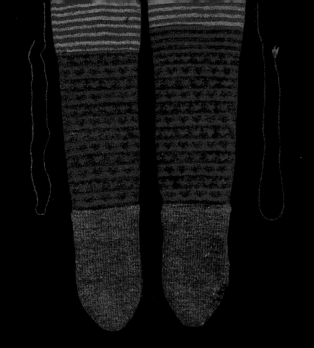

WOMAN'S SOCKS
Kyustendil, western Bulgaria,
mid-20th century

Stocking stitch is used here, with natural
coloured wools. 54 × 16 cm (21¹/₄ × 6¹/₃ in)

WOMAN'S SOCKS
Velingrad, Rodopi Mountains, Bulgaria,
mid-20th century

Hand-knitted, with homespun natural
cream wool. 43.5 × 44 cm (17¹/₄ × 17¹/₃ in)

WOMAN'S SOCKS
Sofia region, Bulgaria,
mid-20th century

Knitted in stocking stitch.
50 × 49.5 cm (19²/₃ × 19¹/₂ in)

THESE SOCKS HAVE BEEN MADE
FROM A MIX OF COMMERCIAL
WOOLS, WHICH ARE MORE SOFTLY
SPUN, AND TIGHTER HOMESPUN
YARNS.

WOMAN'S SOCKS
Pleven, northern Bulgaria, early 20th century

Part of a woman's festive attire, these socks use
a slight variant of the western stocking stitch.
52 × 17 cm (20 1/2 × 6 2/3 in)

WOMAN'S SOCKS
Rodopi Mountains, Bulgaria, mid-20th century

Using polychrome woollen yarns, the socks
are hand-knitted in stocking stitch.
42.5 × 15 cm (16 3/4 × 6 in)

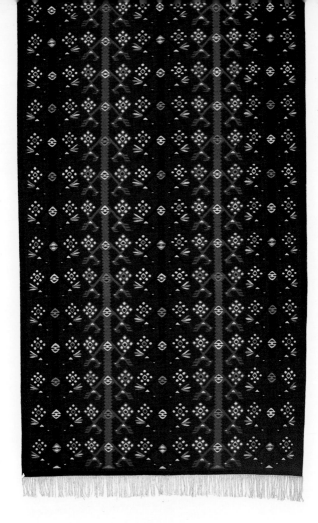

CARPET (*KILIM*)
Chiprovtsi, Bulgaria, early 20th century

The carpet is woven with five large 'tree of life' motifs,
woven on a vertical loom. The ornaments are known as trellis vine (*loznitsa*).
Two green motifs altenate with blue/black trees of life, decorated
with birds sitting above fruit or leaves
319 × 186 cm (125²/₃ × 73¹/₄ in)

THIS IS TYPICAL OF THE CHIPROVTSKI REGION. THE BRIGHTLY
COLOURED STYLIZED PLANT AND BIRD MOTIFS CONTRAST WITH
THE PLAIN BACKGROUND.

WOMAN'S CUMMERBUND
Alexandroupolis district, Thrace, Greece, early 20th century

Worn by the Sarakatsani women, this cummerbund is pieced together with widths
of fabric made using different techniques. It was part of a very elaborate costume:
it would have been worn over a heavy linen chemise and under an embroidered woollen
jacket. Ribbons and braids complement the mix of fabrics.
34 × 155 cm (13^1/$_3$ × 61 in), including outside edge

THE DAZZLING ZIG-ZAG
PATTERN STANDS OUT
AGAINST THE BLACK
TWILL WOVEN CLOTH.

THE CENTRAL SECTION IS
HAS STRIPS OF SILVER- AND
GOLD-COLOURED DASMASK
RIBBON AND BLACK BRAID.

48

WOMAN'S SLEEVELESS COAT
Mirdita region, Albania, mid-20th century

This felted wool everyday coat would have been worn over an embroidered chemise. Made of natural, cream-coloured twill woven wool cloth, it is richly decorated on both the back and the front with couched embroidery. Although red is the prodominant colour, multi-coloured yarns were used.

105 × 47 cm (41$^{1}/_{3}$ × 18$^{1}/_{2}$ in)

THIS MOTIF DEFINES THE SHAPE OF THE WAIST. IT IS USED ON THE LEFT AND RIGHT SIDES OF THE COAT.

MAN'S WAISTCOAT (*MEIDANI*)
Macedonia, Greece, early 20th century

This formal waistcoat would only have been worn by a wealthy person, due to the cost of its silver and gold embroidery. It would have been made from one piece of cloth by a male tailor (*terzidhes*), from the mountainous areas of Greece. Such a garment is part of a long tradition, going back to the 4th century.
29 × 40.5 cm (11¹/₂ × 16 in)

THE VIVID COLOURS OF THE SILK LINING
COMPLEMENT THE ELABORATE EMBROIDERY
AND METAL-WRAPPED THREAD.

WOMAN'S APRON
Bitola region, Former Yugoslav Republic of Macedonia,
mid-20th century

Part of a wedding outfit, the apron is made of two equal-sized pieces of
woven wool cloth joined at the centre (see above). Ribbon and rick rack,
which is made from gold-coloured metal-wrapped thread, are stitched to
the sides. The lower half of the apron is more richly decorated, and
includes coins from the region and heavy woollen fringing.
69 × 56 cm (27 × 22 in)

THE FRINGING CONSISTS OF
SEVERAL LAYERS OF SUBTLY
DIFFERENT SHADES OF RED WOOL,
INTERSPERSED WITH GOLD AND
YELLOW THREAD. THE SEQUINS
AND COINS WOULD HAVE BEEN
ADDED BY LATER GENERATIONS.

WOMAN'S CHEMISE
Bitola region, Former Yugoslav Republic of Macedonia,
mid-20th century

This handwoven cotton cloth is richly decorated with
geometric embroidery at the neckline, cuffs and hem.
Blanket stitch is used on the sleeve edges and hemline.
The rest is stitched in Slav stitch in red, black and
cream, the traditional colours of the region.
111.5 × 80 cm (44 × 31½ in)

THE RED COLOURS COME FROM VEGETABLE DYE
MADE FROM MADDER ROOT. TRANSFERS MAY HAVE
BEEN USED FOR THESE STYLIZED GEOMETRIC SHAPES.
TRADITIONAL DESIGNS SUCH AS THESE WERE OFTEN
PASSED DOWN THROUGH THE GENERATIONS.

WOMAN'S HEADSCARF
Bitola region, Former Yugoslav Republic
of Macedonia, mid-20th century

The finely woven cream-coloured cloth
covers the head and hangs down the back
of the neck. It was an everyday garment,
worn up until the mid-1970s. The tie is
concealed under the fan-shaped cluster
of black cotton threads.
127 × 105 cm (50 × 41½ in)

THIS IS THE ONLY DECORATED AREA OF
THE HEADSCARF. A BLACK VELVET
RIBBON MARKS THE POINT WHERE THE
COTTON THREADS HANG FREELY.

ATHE HEADDRESS HAS A COMPLICATED ARRANGEMENT OF THREADS. THE 'PONYTAIL' IS WRAPPED WITH SOFT RED WOOL AND IS LACED WITH CREAM THREADS. TWO SILVER COINS AND GREEN BEADS ARE SEWN ONTO THE TOP. THE COINS READ '5 LEVA/1930'.

WOMAN'S HEADDRESS
Bitola region, Former Yugoslav Republic of Macedonia, mid-20th century

This elegant rear headdress is made from a length of black plaited wool tied in a 'ponytail' at the back. It would have hung from the top of a jacket and been used to enhance a girl's natural hair. The headdress is hooked onto the shoulders by two diamond-shaped pins.
Length: 80 cm (31 1/2 in)

WOMAN'S CHEMISE
Bitola region, Former Yugoslav Republic of Macedonia, mid-20th century

The orange and black embroidery has very stylized motifs. A later generation would have added the sequins, beadwork and crocheted hem to modernize the garment.
127 × 105 cm (50 × 41 1/2 in)

PINK AND WHITE BRAIDING HAS BEEN ADDED TO THE SLEEVES.

THE MULTCOLOURED THREE-BLOSSOMED MOTIF IS ON EITHER SIDE OF THE HEM.

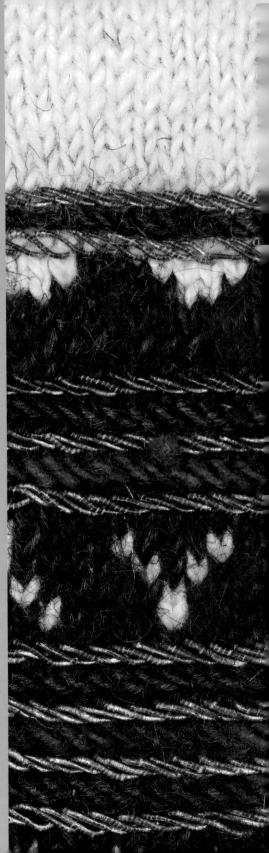

THE CREAM TOPS OF THE SOCKS, WITH
THEIR DELICATE RIBBED EDGING, WOULD
HAVE BEEN HIDDEN UNDER THE HEM OF
THE CHEMISE.

WOMAN'S SOCKS
Former Yugoslav Republic of Macedonia,
mid-20th century

Socks worn by nomadic Vlach people
were knitted on round needles using
white, red, blue and black wool, and
gold-coloured metal-wrapped thread.
53 × 14 cm (21 × 5$^{1}/_{2}$ in)

THE COLOURS OF THE APRON MATCHED
THOSE OF THE SOCKS (LEFT). HOWEVER, THE
PATTERNS ARE VERY DIFFERENT. WHILE
CROSSES ARE USED ON THE SOCKS, THE
DIAMOND MOTIF IS USED ON THE APRON.

WOMAN'S APRON
Former Yugoslav Republic of Macedonia,
mid-20th century

The Vlach people made this pleated apron
from two equal-sized pieces of woven wool
cloth. Gathered into a band at the waist,
it has been worked in dark red, green, blue
and black wool, as well as gold and silver
metal-wrapped thread.
26.5 × 23.5 cm ($10^1/_2$ × $9^1/_4$ in)

WOMAN'S COAT
Galičnik, Former Yugoslav Republic of Macedonia,
mid-20th century

This forms part of the wedding outfit of a Mijaksi woman.
The women spun and wove the sheep's wool into cloth, while
the men made it into felt and tailored it into a coat. This
would have been worn on top of a chemise and two small
jackets, all with gold filigree buttons.
101 × 48 cm (39²/₃ × 19 in)

THE HEAVY COAT HAS MANY LAYERS. FALSE
SLEEVES HANG OVER HEAVILY DECORATED
SLEEVES (RIGHT), WHICH WERE ATTACHED
TO THE CHEMISE.

WOMAN'S CHEMISE SLEEVE
Galičnik, Former Yugoslav Republic of
Macedonia, mid-20th century

This is the detachable part of the Mijaksi
woman's wedding outfit (left). The sleeves were
detachable so that the chemise could be washed.
Over this longer sleeve was a shorter sleeve
with fringing. It covered the upper arm.
101 × 48 cm (39³/₄ × 19 in)

RED AND MAROON BANDS ALTERNATE
WITH DIAMOND-PATTERNED OPENWORK,
WITH DECORATIVE MOTIFS USING MULTI-
COLOURED THREADS.

DECORATIVE TOWEL
Skopje region, Former Yugoslav Republic of Macedonia, mid 20th-century

Towels such as this were usually given as gifts at a wedding
ceremony. It would have been tucked into a man's belt,
as part of his festive summer attire.
92 × 26 cm (26¼ × 10¼ in)

THE MULTICOLOURED GEOMETRIC MOTIFS MAY BE BASED ON BIRDS.

THE MAIN FABRIC IS A CHEQUERED
WOVEN WOOL CLOTH. THE FRONT
PANEL IS EXTREMELY ELABORATE,
INCORPORATING A MIXTURE OF
APPLIED MATERIALS.

WOMAN'S SLEEVELESS COAT
Skopje region, Former Yugoslav Republic of Macedonia,
mid-20th century

This coat would have been worn as part of a woman's festive summer attire.
It is made of woven wool cloth, which would have been purchased from travelling
merchants. Although the material is used as economically as possible,
it still achieves a very elegant silhouette.
89 × 83 cm (35 × 32²/₃ in)

WOMAN'S SOCKS
Belgrade, Serbia, mid-20th century

Hand-knitted with dark blue wool yarn
and a floral patterning, these socks
would have been for everyday wear.
47 × 13 cm (18 1/2 × 5 1/4 in)

THE PART OF THE SOCK COVERING THE
CALVES IS HIGHLY TEXTURED AND
WOULD HAVE BEEN VISIBLE BELOW
THE CHEMISE.

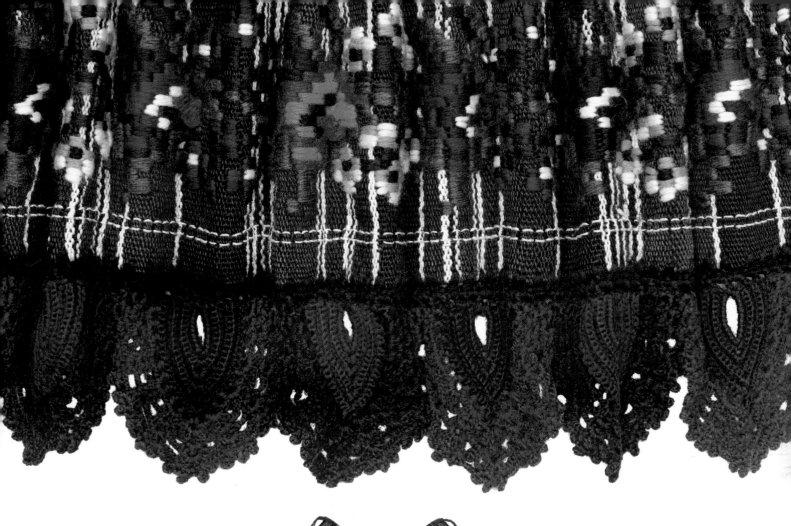

BACK APRON
Belgrade, Serbia, 1930s

The apron would be tied on inside out, and arranged to reveal the emboidery. The bottom two corners are pulled up and tucked under the cord at the back to create a butterfuly shape. The hem embroidery then hangs down vertically (as on p. 16).
89 × 60 cm (35 × 23²/₃ in)

THE CLOTH IS GATHERED AT THE WAIST AND THE SCALLOPED CROCHETED EDGES EXENTUATE THE GATHERED PLEATS.

WOMAN'S APRON (*FUTA*)
Skopje region, Former Yugoslav Republic of Macedonia,
mid-20th century

The apron ties pull in the material, so that when worn
the apron is gathered at the top. It is made in tapestry weave
using goat hair thread, which would have been woven by
women in the village and dyed by the men.
64 × 69 cm (25 $\frac{1}{4}$ × 27 $\frac{1}{4}$ in)

AGAINST A BRILLIANT RED BACKGROUND, THE LARGE DIAMONDS CONTAIN COLOURFUL MOTIFS, WHICH ARE ALL
SLIGHTLY DIFFERENT. BLACK CHEVRONS AND WHITE ZIG-ZAGS PROVIDE A LIVELY SURROUND TO EACH DIAMOND.

IN CLUSTERS OF THE SAME
COLOUR, THE POMPOMS ARE
STITCHED TO A LACE BORDER
ALONG THE SIDES AND
HEMLINE OF THE APRON.

WOMAN'S APRON
Vevčani, near Ohrid, Former Yugoslav Republic of Macedonia, 1920s

As with the apron on pp. 72–3, the ties gather the material at the top
when the apron is worn. The range of colours that has been stitched onto
the main body of the apron is also used for the pompoms.
74 × 76.5 cm (29 1/4 × 30 in)

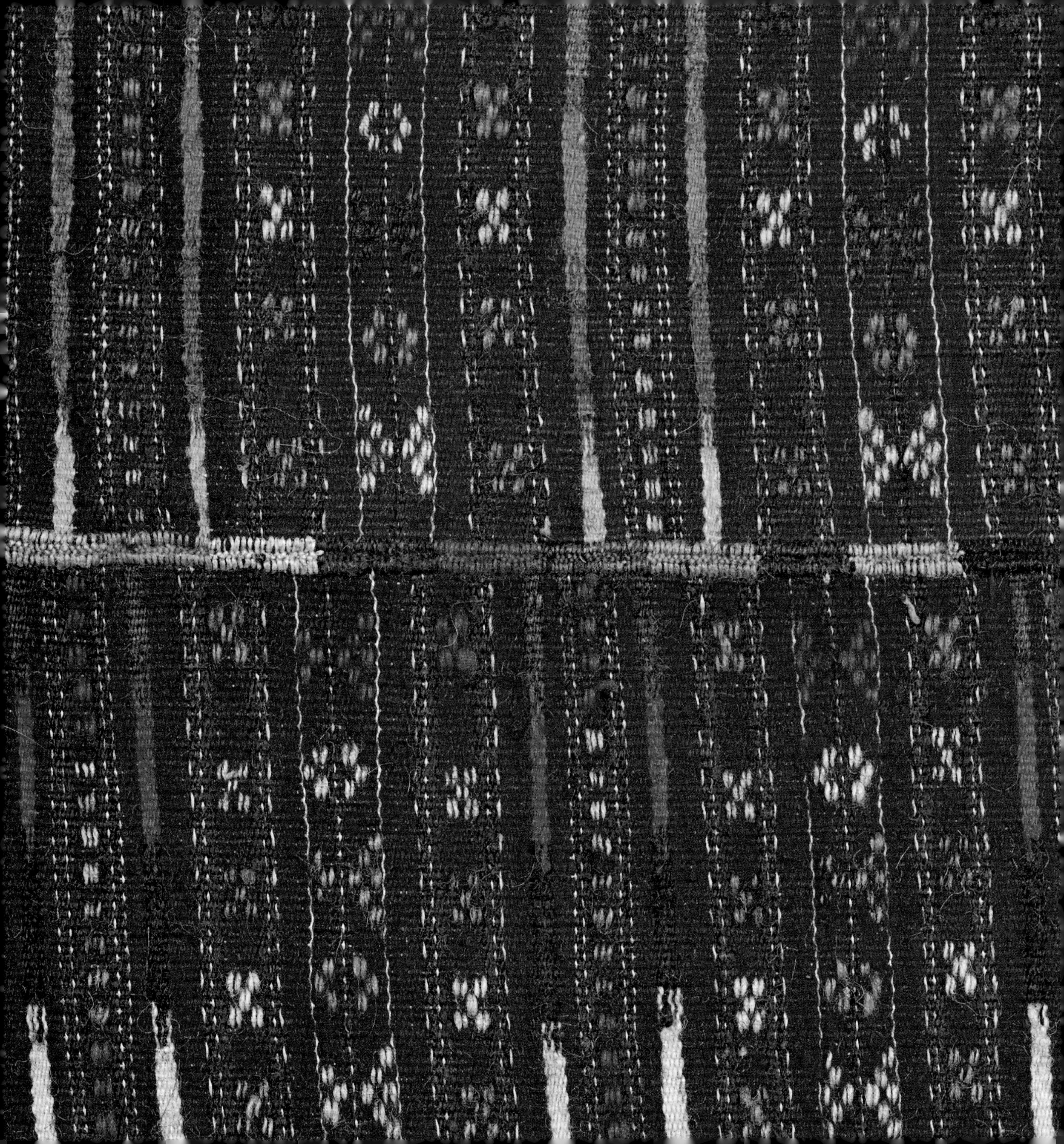

THE FRONT PANEL IS AN ELABORATE WORKING OF STYLIZED FLORAL MOTIFS AND UNDULATING LINES, STITCHED IN SILVER-COLOURED METAL-WRAPPED THREAD. THIS CONTRASTS WITH THE RICH PURPLE COTTON VELVET CLOTH.

NARROW ORANGE/RED VERTICAL STRIPES CREATE AN ATTRACTIVE PATTERN AGAINST THE DARK BLUE BACKGROUND OF WOVEN CLOTH.

WOMAN'S JACKET
Vevčani, near Ohrid, Former Yugoslav Republic of
Macedonia, 1920s

This sleeveless and flared jacket is made from woven cotton
cloth, and is quilted and lined. At a later date, a 6 mm ($^1/_2$ in)
strip of floral printed cloth has been added to the hem,
along with a strip of blue cotton rick rack.
100 × 102 cm (39 $^1/_3$ × 40 $^1/_4$ in)

WOMAN'S BIB (*PLASTRON*)
Debar, Former Yugoslav Republic of
Macedonia, mid-20th century

This decorative bib would have been worn under
a chemise and tied around the neck. It has been
cut out of a rectangular piece of natural cream
woven cloth, and then an heavily embroidered
panel has been added.
43 × 33 cm (17 × 13 in)

THE STRIKING PATTERN OF THE EMBROIDERY HAS BEEN
WORKED IN ORANGE, YELLOW AND BLUE/BLACK WOOL.

WOMAN'S SOCKS
Debar, Former Yugoslav Republic of
Macedonia, mid-20th century

These attractively patterned socks have been
hand-knitted, using the technique of stranded
knitting. Cream, yellow, green and black wool
yarns have been used alongside the more
dominant orange.
52 × 16.5 cm (20 1/2 × 6 1/2 in)

THESE SOCKS HAVE BEEN DESIGNED WITH IDENTICAL
GEOMETRIC PATTERNING ON EACH SIDE OF THE FOOT.

WOMAN'S CHEMISE
Skopje Black Mountain
region, Former Yugoslav
Republic of Macedonia,
early 20th century

In *Black Lamb and Grey
Falcon*, Rebecca West,
travelling in Macedonia in the
1930s, said of this region:
'They wear the most dignified
and beautiful dresses of any
of the Balkans, gowns of
coarse linen embroidered with
black wool in designs using
the Christian symbols, which
are at once abstract (being
entirely unrepresentational)
and charged with
passionate feeling.'
125 × 160 cm (49 $\frac{1}{4}$ × 63 in)

BLACK AND BLUE COUNTED
THREAD EMBROIDERY EXTENDS
THE WHOLE LENGTH OF EACH
SLEEVE. REBECCEA WEST WAS
VERY STRUCK BY THE USE OF
BLUE IN SUCH GARMENTS,
DESCRIBING IT AS GIVING 'THE
EFFECT OF AN INNER LIGHT
BURNING IN THE HEAT OF
DARKNESS'.

glossary

These definitions relate to the Balkan examples in this book

Aniline dyes also known as chemical dyes or synthetic dyes, introduced in the mid 19th century; give a much wider range of colours than could be achieved with vegetable dyes, and some are fast when washed

Chain stitch each new stitch is drawn through the previous one, thus forming a chain

Chemise long shirt that forms the undergarment for most women's costumes; it is usually made of cotton or linen and often heavily embroidered on the parts that are seen

Couching a method of sewing down a thick thread, bunch of threads, cord or gold with small stitches, at regular intervals, in a thinner thread

Crochet a kind of chaining whereby the yarn is looped vertically and horizontally through two (or more) loops using a special needle with a small hook on the end

Cross stitch an embroidery stitch where the ground threads are counted to make the pattern and the thread is crossed from left to right and top to bottom

Damask a self-patterned satin-weave fabric taking its name from the city of Damascus where it first came to Western notice. Satin weave refers to the way the warp and weft threads are combined to produce a shimmering effect when the light falls on the vertical and horizontal threads. In the Balkans it would have been obtained from merchants travelling through the area

Drawn threadwork an openwork technique whereby individual threads are removed from the cloth and the remaining threads are strengthened by binding, usually with other embroidery threads

Flax the plant that provides the raw fibres for linen; the fibres are washed, beaten and hung or laid out in the sun to bleach

Garter stitch the simplest form of horizontal ribbing in which knit rows alternate with purl rows

Gunche or **gounche** a sleeveless white woollen garment, open down the front and slightly flared

Horizontal loom where the warp is stretched horizontally across vertical supports and the warp threads extend from front to back; as alternative threads are raised and lowered the weft is passed from side to side across the warp

Knotted stitch the thread, often of thick wool or coarse yarn, is pulled through the cloth and twisted into a knot

Loznitsa a trellis vine ornamentation

Openwork see drawn and pulled threadwork

Pulled threadwork an openwork technique created by teasing threads of the ground fabric apart (but not removing them) and binding the remaining threads together

Rick rack machine-woven braid in a meander or zigzag pattern

Roughing machine a machine used to make felt from fleece

Selvedge side edge of a fabric where the weft returns

Straight stitch single stitches, sometimes of varying size, with a space between each

Stranded knitting a technique for working two colours of yarn in the same row and involves carrying two different yarns at the same time. The yarn that is not being used is carried across the back of the work, leaving a 'strand' of yarn where it has not been knitted

Stocking stitch (also known as stockinette stitch) the most basic knitted fabric; every stitch (as seen from the right side) is a knit stitch

Supplementary weft a technique of applying decorative effects to a fabric by inserting additional weft threads during weaving

Tablet loom a small simple hand-held loom used to make belts or other narrow pieces of cloth. The warps are threaded through small tablets or cards pierced with holes and tensioned at either end. The tablets are rotated, either in groups or singly, to form different weaving sheds for the wefts to pass through

Tapestry a weave for creating designs in cloth with a weft composed of threads of different colours, which do not pass from selvage to selvage but are carried back and forth, interweaving only with the part of the warp that is required for a particular pattern area

Terzidhes male tailors from Greece

Twill fabric each passage of the weft through the warps goes over two, under one, over two, under one. In the next passage, the same sequence is repeated but staggered, to produce diagonal lines on the face of the cloth. Variations can create different patterns such as herringbone

Vertical loom an upright loom where the warp is stretched vertically. In the Balkans, it is used for carpet making, usually done by women on a loom in their own house

Warp threads that stretch lengthways in a fabric as woven

Weft threads that stretch widthways in the fabric as woven and interlace with the warp

selected reading

There is a wealth of literature in the Balkan languages, but this list is restricted principally to publications in the English language.

Allcock, J. and Young, A., *Black Lambs and Grey Falcons: Women Travellers in the Balkans*. Bradford University Press, Bradford, 1991

Broufas, C., 'Introduction to Greek costumes' in A. Raftis, *Forty Greek Costumes from the Dora Stratou Collection*. Dora Stratou Theatre, Athens, 1996

Burnham, D.K., *Warp and Weft: A Textile Terminology*. Royal Ontario Museum, Toronto, 1980

Clabburn, P, *The Needleworker's Dictionary*. Macmillan, London, 1976

Durham, E. M., *High Albania*, Edward Arnold, London, 1909

Gjergji, A., *Albanian Folk Costumes* (*Veshje popullore shqiptare*), 3 vols. Instituti i Kulturës Popullore, Tirenë. Vol. 1, 1999; vol. 2 by M. Tirta, A. Dojaka and Y. Selimi, 2001; vol. 3, 2004

Hatzimichali, A., *The Greek Folk Costume*, vols I and II. Benaki Museum, Athens, 1977. These comprehensive volumes are based on the outstanding collection of Greek costumes and textiles in the Benaki Museum.

Hill, J. 'Edith Durham as a Collector', in Allcock and Young, 1991 (see previous entry)

Hodgson, J., 'Edith Durham, Traveller and Publicist', in Allcock and Young, 1991 (see previous entry)

Kwasnik, E. (ed), *British and Bulgarian Ethnography*. National Museums and Galleries on Merseyside, 1992. Papers from a symposium in Liverpool, October 1989.

Macdermott, M., *Bulgarian Folk Customs*. Jessica Kingsley Publishers, London and Philadelphia, 1998

Paine, S., *Embroidered Textiles: Traditional Patterns from Five Continents*. Thames and Hudson, London, 1990. Revised and expanded 2008

Pantelic, N., *Traditional Arts and Crafts in Yugoslavia*. Belgrade, 1984

Papantaniou, J., *Macedonian Costumes*. Peloponnesian Folklore Foundation, Nafplion, 1992

Papantaniou, J., *Greek Regional Costumes*. Peloponnesian Folklore Foundation, Nafplion, 1996

Rosslyn, F., 'Rebecca West, Gerda and the Sense of Process', in Allcock and Young, 1991 (see previous entry)

Vasileva, V., 'Embroidery in Traditional Bulgarian Folk Costume', in Kwasnik, E., 1992 (see previous entry)

Vasileva-Toderova, M., 'The Present state of the Bulgarian Folk Wedding', in Kwasnik, E., 1992

West, R., *Black Lamb and Grey Falcon*. Penguin Books, London, 1941, new edition with introduction by Geoff Dyer, 2007

Zora, P., *Introduction and Catalogue: Exhibition of Greek Folk Art*. Museum of Greek Folk Art, Athens, 1976
Embroideries and Jewellery of Greek National Costumes, Museum of Greek Folk Art, Athens, 1981

Zunic-Bas, L., *Folk Traditions in Yugoslavia*. Izdavacki Zavod, Yugoslavia, 1967

The website of the Embroiderers Guild has several stitch drawings and descriptions which are very helpful: http://www.embroiderersguild.com/stitch/stitches/index.html

museum accession numbers

Each number begins with the year of acquisition, followed by the donor or vendor.

PAGE	ACC. NO.
1	Eu1995,04.9
2	Eu1971,01.135
	Given by the Bulgarian Committee for Cultural Relations
4	Eu1995,03.13
	Given by Mercia MacDermott
5	Eu1997,04.38
	Given by Ken Ward
6	Eu1971,01.59
	Given by the Bulgarian Committee for Cultural Relations
7	Eu1971,01.6
	Given by the Bulgarian Committee for Cultural Relations
23	Eu1914,0619.3a and b
	Given by Mary Edith Durham
24	Eu1973,01.6
	Acquired from Mrs J.G. Davies
25	Eu1973,01.7
	Acquired from Mrs J.G. Davies
26	Eu1993,07.31
	Diane Waller collection
27	Eu1993,07.32
	Diane Waller collection
28–9	Eu1998,05.6
	Acquired from Roberto Busati
30–31	Eu2003,02.13
	Given by Stephanie Schwandner-Sievers
32–3	Eu1971,01.13
	Given by the Bulgarian Committee for Cultural Relations
34–5	Eu1971,01.6
	Given by the Bulgarian Committee for Cultural Relations
36–7	Eu1971,01.16
	Given by the Bulgarian Committee for Cultural Relations
38–9	Eu1971,01.37
	Given by the Bulgarian Committee for Cultural Relations
40–41	Eu1971,01.43
	Given by the Bulgarian Committee for Cultural Relations
42–3	Eu1971,01.59
	Given by the Bulgarian Committee for Cultural Relations
44–5 (left to right)	Eu1993,07.39 Diane Waller collection
	Eu1995,03.13 Given by Mercia MacDermott
	Eu1995,03.2 Given by Mercia MacDermott
	Eu1995,04.18 Given by Mrs Protitch Moreggio
	Eu1995,03.23 Given by Mercia MacDermott
46–7	Eu1971,01.135
	Given by the Bulgarian Committee for Cultural Relations
48–9	Eu1971,03.8
	Acquired from Dimitri Papadimos
50–51	Eu2003,03.2
	Given by Erika Tappe
52–3	Eu2006,0904.5
	Given by Dr H. P. Livas-Dawes
54–5	Eu1993,07.14
	Diane Waller collection
56–7	Eu1993,07.18
	Diane Waller collection
58	Eu1993,07.52
	Diane Waller collection
59	Eu2001,01.43
	Diane Waller collection
61	Eu1993,07.56
	Diane Waller collection
62	Eu1994,01.3
	Diane Waller collection
63	Eu1994,01.6
	Diane Waller collection
64	Eu1997,04.131
	Given by Ken Ward
65	Eu1997,04.129
	Given by Ken Ward
66–7	Eu1994,01.22
	Diane Waller collection
68–9	Eu1994,01.26
	Diane Waller collection
70	Eu1997,04.38
	Given by Ken Ward
71	Eu1997,04.33
	Given by Ken Ward
72–3	Eu1997,04.115
	Given by Ken Ward
74–5	Eu1998,02.27
	Diane Waller collection
76–7	Eu1998,02.33
	Diane Waller collection
78	Eu2001,01.13
	Diane Waller collection
79	Eu2001,01.12
	Diane Waller collection
80–81	Eu2001,02.1
	Given by Diane Waller
Cover	Eu1971,01.37
	Given by the Bulgarian Committee for Cultural Relations
Inside cover	Eu1993,07.56
	Diane Waller collection

author's acknowledgements

Grateful thanks to colleagues at the British Museum who have helped in the selection of items and in preparing the book – in particular Sem Longhurst, Tay Keen, Helen Wolfe, Judy Rudoe, Imogen Laing, Ray Watkins, Coralie Hepburn, Caroline Brooke Johnson, Miranda Harrison, Vicki Robinson and Pippa Cruikshank; to Michael Row for taking the photos; Nina Shandloff for causing the book to happen; to Sarah Posey; to Mercia MacDermott for her intimate knowledge of the Balkans, and for lending photographs for the introduction. Also to Ken Ward, leader of the Zivko Firfov Dance Group; to Dmitri Feary and members of Balkansko Oro in Oxford; to Linda Baguley for sharing many adventures and for lending photographs; and to the people I met in the Balkans throughout the past forty years, who generously gave time, books and even items of costume when hearing of my interest.

This book is in memory of my husband, Dani Lumley, leader of the Vasil Levsky Bulgarian Dance Group with whom I shared most of my journeys in the Balkans, and our dear friend, Christo Stoyanov, an inspired dancer.

picture credits

index